Theme park science

HIGH SPEED THRILLS

By Nathan Lepora

ticktock

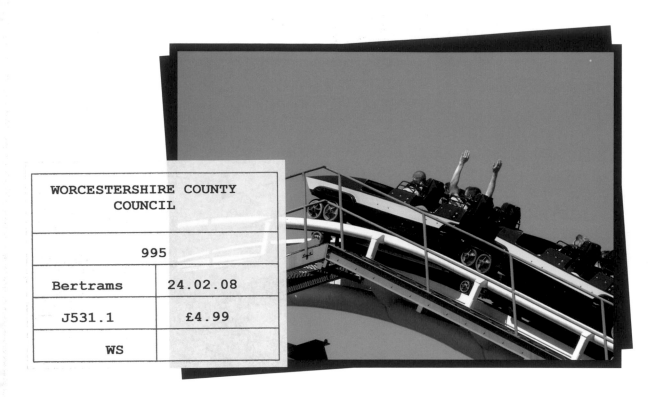

First published in Great Britain in 2008 by ticktock Media Ltd,
2 Orchard Business Centre, North Farm Road, Tunbridge Wells, Kent, TN2 3XF

ticktock project editor: Sophie Furse
ticktock picture researcher: Lizzie Knowles
ticktock project designer: Hayley Terry
With thanks to: Carol Ryback, Justin Spain, and Suzy Gazlay

ISBN 978 1 84696 612 5 pbk

Printed in China

CONTENTS

What makes roller coasters so much fun? Maybe it is that feeling of your stomach floating up inside of you. These feelings are **forces** pushing against you. Forces push or pull objects to change their **speed** or direction.

THE FUN OF PUSHES AND PULLS

Roller coasters use constantly changing forces to make the ride fun. The basic design is very simple. Riders sit in cars that roll along fixed **tracks**. As the cars travel the tracks, they go up, down, turn and twist around at varying speeds.

Each swerve, spin, and loop digs the car wheels into the tracks. This causes the tracks to react by pushing back against the wheels. The sideways force of the tracks pushing back against the wheels stops the cars from flying off the tracks.

Forces also act on the people inside the cars. As the cars twist and turn around the course they push and pull against the riders. This is why you feel squashed and jostled on a roller coaster.

THAT'S AMAZING!

Roller coasters can produce a force that feels like four people sitting on you!

KNOW YOUR FORCES

All forces cause a change in shape, speed, or direction. Forces have different names. The name explains what the force does.

START

FRICTION

Friction slows and finally stops the cars at the finish. **Friction** may work gradually. It can also stop the car suddenly. A slowing speed is called **deceleration**.

Centripetal force is the sideways force you feel as the cars swerve around corners. The forces of **acceleration** and gravity work with or against each other through the turns.

CENTRIPETAL FORCE

Inertia keeps you moving along your path until another force changes your speed or direction. It is not a force, but a property of how an object moves.

ACCELERATING FORCE

Accelerating force makes the waiting roller coaster cars start moving, or makes a moving car speed up.

GRAVITATIONAL FORCE

Gravitational force constantly pulls everything toward Earth. **Gravity** makes the cars go faster and faster as they fall. It combines with acceleration to make you feel heavier as the roller coaster cars go uphill.

CHAPTER 2: SPEED AND VELOCITY

On a roller coaster the world whooshes past as you speed along. Speed is how fast an object moves. Two factors determine speed – the distance an object travels and the time it takes to travel that distance.

SPEED AND DISTANCE

Faster objects travel further than slower objects within the same time period. Imagine two cars racing on a track. The car with greater speed will travel the distance in less time and win.

5 metres per second

10 metres per second

The blue car wins the race shown in this diagram because its speed is greater.

FAST AND SAFE

The fastest roller coaster on Earth is the awesome **Kingda Ka** in New Jersey, USA. Riders hurtle at a terrifying speed of 206 kilometres per hour. At this speed, the cars are shooting past a distance of six school buses in a row in just one second!

High speeds make roller coaster rides thrilling. Controlling their speed makes them safe. Engineers carefully design the hills, bends, twists, and dips to give riders a safe and exciting experience.

THAT'S AMAZING!

Kingda Ka is a whopping 139 metres high, making it the world's tallest roller coaster.

WHAT IS VELOCITY?

Velocity is a combination of an object's speed and the direction it is moving. For example, if you move at the same speed straight ahead, then to your right, and finally to your left, your velocity has changed with each move.

On a roller coaster, velocity can be more useful than speed to give you a thrill. At certain places along the track you may be moving at the same speed. However, the direction of the track causes changes in velocity that make the world spin in exciting ways around you.

A tight bend on the Goliath roller coaster in Atlanta, Georgia, USA. Velocity changes direction through a bend.

Zooming through a turn on a roller coaster helps show how speed and velocity differ. The car's speed stays the same while swerving through the corner. But its velocity – the direction it takes before, during, and after each part of the turn – changes.

THE VELOCITY ARROW

A good way to imagine velocity is as a pointing arrow. This arrow shows the direction in which an object is moving. Whenever the object moves in a new direction, its velocity arrow turns to point the new way.

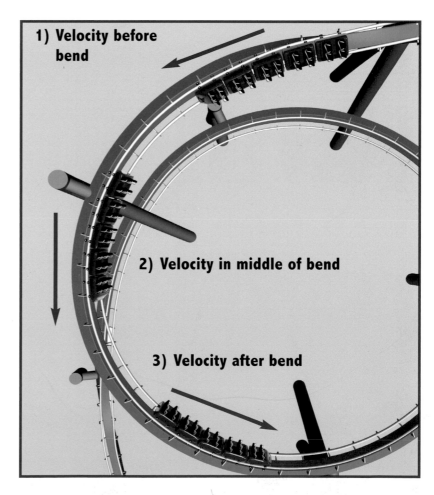

1) Velocity before bend

2) Velocity in middle of bend

3) Velocity after bend

Part of the fun of roller coasters is speeding up and slowing down. A change in speed is an acceleration. When speeding up, you accelerate. As you slow down, you decelerate.

HOW ROLLER COASTERS ACCELERATE

Roller coasters use hills for acceleration and deceleration. A car rolling down a hill accelerates to faster speeds. A car travelling up the next hill decelerates to slower speeds.

The layout of a roller coaster is very carefully planned. Designers place the hills to perfectly control the speed and acceleration throughout the entire ride. They even play tricks by making the ride feel dangerous and out of control when it is safe!

BOOMERANG ROLLER COASTERS

Some roller coasters shoot back like a **boomerang**! Halfway through the ride, you reach a steep slope. The deceleration slows you to a stop. Then you roll back. The whole ride flashes past you backward until you reach the starting point.

This is Déjà Vu, a giant boomerang roller coaster in Atlanta, Georgia, USA.

From the start, the cars are pulled backward up to point A, then dropped face down, zooming along the ride until reaching point B. Then as the riders look up at the sky, they are dropped backwards down the track to hurtle back along the ride to the start.

WHICH IS THE FASTEST?

How can you guess which is the fastest roller coaster in any theme park?

The tallest roller coaster in any theme park usually reaches the greatest speeds. The roller coaster cars continue to accelerate as they roll down a hill. Taller hills provide a longer track for greater acceleration on the downslope.

The stomach-churning drop on Dodonpa, a roller coaster at Fujiyoshida, Japan.

THAT'S AMAZING!

Dodonpa accelerates to 172 kilometres per hour in just 77 metres – it's like taking off in a jet fighter!

CATAPULT LAUNCHES

A **catapult** is another way to accelerate a roller coaster to super speeds. A catapult is a device that shoots the ride forward from standing still.

The catapult on the Japanese roller coaster **Dodonpa** gives the most acceleration of any roller coaster on Earth.

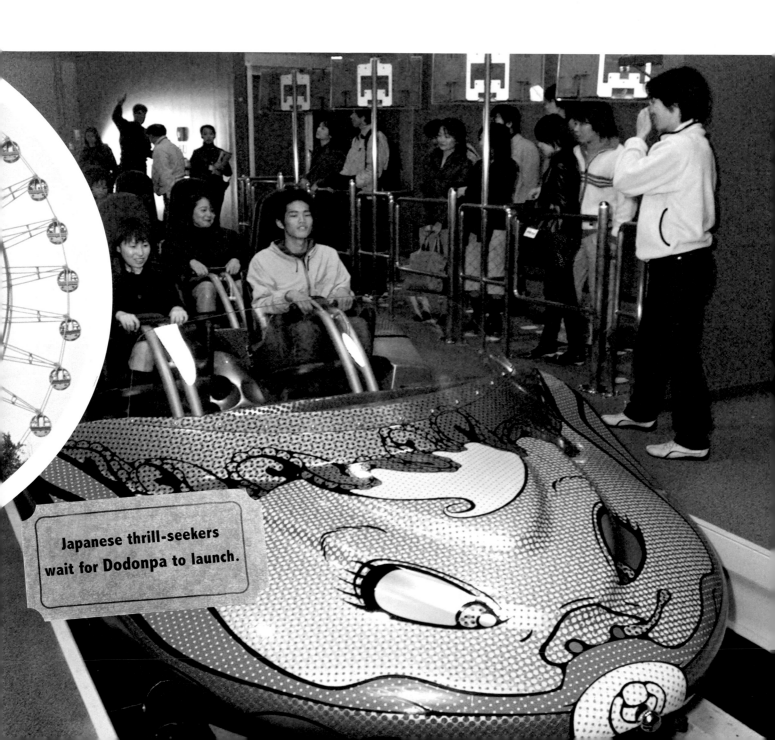

Japanese thrill-seekers wait for Dodonpa to launch.

Mass is the amount of matter in an object. The larger the **mass** of an object, the more force it takes to move it or stop it.

WHAT IS MASS?

Mass makes objects difficult to move. Imagine kicking a lead ball and a hollow plastic ball of the same size. The lead ball would hardly budge, but you would probably kick the plastic ball pretty far. The lead ball has a greater mass for its size.

Roller coaster cars are large and made out of metal. A roller coaster train full of people needs an enormous push to start moving. You hear this motor roar as the ride starts.

THAT'S AMAZING!

Even when empty, a train of six cars can have the same mass as an elephant.

A huge motor under the tracks provides the push that starts a roller coaster moving.

WHAT IS INERTIA?

Bumper cars need a push to start them moving. Once a car starts moving, it keeps travelling in a straight line. Only another force (such as another bumper car) can make the car speed up, slow down or change direction.

Inertia is a property of how something moves that makes it resist having its movement changed. An object with greater mass is more difficult to accelerate because of its inertia. It needs more force to stop, start or change speed.

BUMPER CARS!

Bumper cars work using inertia. Riders drive around in little cars that crash into each other. The force of one car bashing into another car knocks it out of the way.

What would happen if you crashed your bumper car into one ridden by two larger adults? The adults have greater mass, and therefore need more force to move them. Your car would probably just bounce off their car – which would hardly move!

English scientist and mathematician Sir Isaac Newton (1642–1727) discovered the laws for how objects move.

BEFORE COLLISION

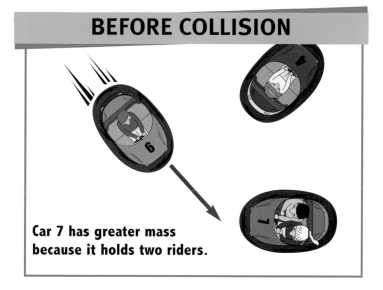

Car 7 has greater mass because it holds two riders.

COLLISION

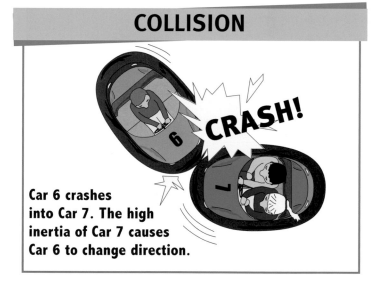

Car 6 crashes into Car 7. The high inertia of Car 7 causes Car 6 to change direction.

AFTER COLLISION

Car 7 continues in the same direction as before, but Car 6 has now changed direction.

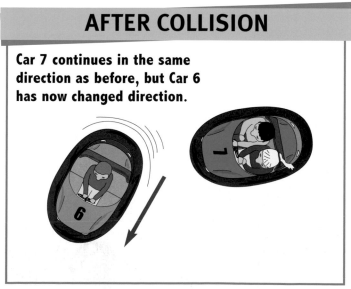

Roller coaster cars ride on wheels that roll over metal tracks. The tracks guide the cars of the ride.

THE FIRST ROLLER COASTER

Old roller coasters are like trains. Each train car rides on grooved wheels that fit onto two metal rails. Josiah White built the first American roller coaster in 1829 in Mauch Chunk, Philadelphia. Even though he built it to carry coal, people liked to ride in it instead!

Old-fashioned roller coasters have wooden frames. Some people prefer roller coasters with wooden support structures. The wood makes the cars sway more than steel frames do!

The swaying of the tracks helps to absorb the force of the cars travelling over it.

Steel rails

Steel wheels and axles

Laminated wood track

MODERN ROLLER COASTERS

Roller coasters today are high-tech structures made from curved steel. The tracks are steel tubes that twist the ride through amazing turns. Specially designed wheels roll over the tracks. These wheels fit onto the top, bottom, and sides of the tracks.

THAT'S AMAZING!

The first roller coasters were ice slides with sledges. Even famous people like Russian Empress, Catherine the Great (1729–1796) enjoyed them!

The twists and turns of the Superman Krypton roller coaster at Six Flags Fiesta, Texas, USA.

Roller coasters are always slowing down because of **friction** against their tracks. Friction is a force that resists movement. The rougher the surface a moving object rubs against, the greater the friction.

FRICTIONAL FORCE

When two surfaces rub, they cause friction. Every surface is covered in microscopic ridges – even if it looks smooth. As the ridges move over each other, they catch and push against the movement.

Friction is the force that acts on an object's surfaces. It causes deceleration, or a slowing of movement.

EFFECTS OF FRICTION

It is thrilling to go fast. But friction slows you down. Friction is always at work between the tracks and wheels of a roller coaster car. Too much friction might even trap riders in a dip!

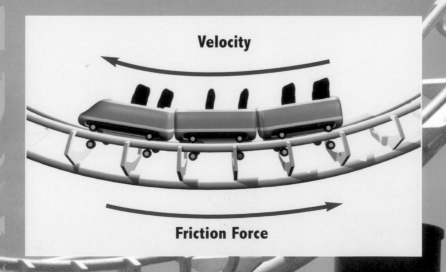

Velocity

Friction Force

MAGNETIC TRAINS

This Japanese **maglev** train hovers above its tracks using magnetic power to avoid friction. In the future, roller coasters might do this, too!

Maglev trains can go much faster than other trains and can reach speeds of 581 kilometres per hour.

SMOOTH RIDES

Roller coaster designers have clever ways to make rides feel quicker and smoother. They design the wheels and tracks to cause less friction. This makes the cars glide along and, more importantly, go faster!

GUIDING AROUND TURNS

Many roller coasters have three types of wheels. Running wheels and upstop wheels fit above and below the tracks. Guide wheels run against the sides of the tracks. Guide wheels take over during turns to smooth the ride and cause less friction.

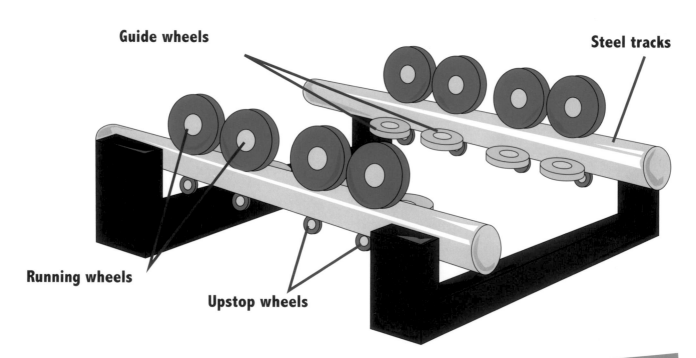

Guide wheels

Steel tracks

Running wheels

Upstop wheels

SUPER-SMOOTH WHEELS

New roller coasters have wheels coated in high-tech plastics. This covering makes the wheels much smoother than if they were just metal. The coated wheels quietly glide over the tracks to reach super-fast speeds.

THAT'S AMAZING!

The smooth covering on the wheels of high-tech roller coasters is also used to coat jet aircraft.

TUBULAR TRACKS

Modern roller coasters run on special tracks made from steel tubes. The tubes' twists and turns add to the ride's excitement. The steel tubes are also very smooth. They cause less friction so the ride goes faster.

Wicked Twister at Cedar Point, Ohio, USA zooms riders around at speeds of 115 kilometres per hour.

Air rushes past you when you ride on a roller coaster. This rush of air also slows down the car. **Air resistance** is friction between air and an object. Air pushes against moving objects to slow them down.

PUSHY AIR

On a windy day you feel air pushing against you. Air is made of billions of tiny particles that bump into you. When you move fast, you bump against air. It pushes against you to slow you down.

STREAMLINING FOR SPEED

A sleek shape cuts easily through air. For example, jet aircraft and racing cars have smooth, pointy, **streamlined** shapes. Air rushes past them without causing much friction.

The fastest roller coasters also have sleek designs to reduce air resistance. Their front cars are shaped to cut through air. This streamlined shape allows them to reach super-fast speeds. It also protects people from tornado-force winds created by the speeding ride.

THAT'S AMAZING!

Parachutes glide slowly and gently to Earth because of air resistance.

Brakes are devices that use friction to slow something down. Most **brakes** act like a sort of clamp that fits onto a wheel. When you tighten the clamp, it rubs against the wheel to cause friction.

SLAM ON THE BRAKES

Every wheeled vehicle needs a way to stop moving. Brakes are designed to cause friction when desired. Brakes add to the fun of the ride: think of the screeching stop as a roller coaster ride ends.

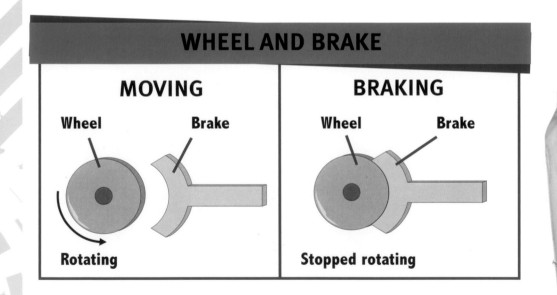

WHEEL AND BRAKE

MOVING

Wheel   Brake

Rotating

BRAKING

Wheel   Brake

Stopped rotating

THAT'S AMAZING!

Some ultra-modern roller coasters use magnetic brakes. Force from huge **magnets** stops the ride.

STOPPING ROLLER COASTERS

Brakes do not have to use rough clamps to work. Air resistance is used for braking on airplanes – flaps lift up on the wings to provide friction against air. **Magnetism** is also used in some brakes to slow down metal objects.

Roller coaster cars do not have brakes! Do not worry though – brakes are built into the tracks. They clamp onto metal fins that hang beneath the cars.

ROLLER COASTER BRAKE

MOVING

BRAKING

SCREECH!

Fin

Brake

Fin

Brake

Acceleration is a change in speed as time passes. An object that is gaining speed is accelerating. An object whose speed is decreasing is decelerating. *(see also deceleration)*

Air resistance is friction between an object and air. It makes the object travel slower. *(see also friction and streamlined)*

Boomerang roller coasters are roller coasters designed to return to the start by rolling backward halfway through the ride.

Brakes are devices that use friction to slow or stop an object. *(see also friction)*

Catapults are devices that launch a roller coaster ride from its starting point to an almost immediate high speed. This is instead of pulling it up a lift-hill.

Centripetal forces are forces that pull an object toward the centre as it travels in a circle.

Deceleration is a decrease in speed over time; the opposite of acceleration. *(see also acceleration)*

Forces are pushes or pulls that change the shape, speed, or direction of an object.

Friction is a force that slows or resists movement. Rough surfaces cause higher amounts of friction than smooth surfaces. *(see also streamlined)*

Gravity is the force that pulls one mass toward another. An object with a large mass has more gravity than an object with a smaller mass. Gravity also causes falling objects to accelerate as they fall toward Earth.

Inertia is the tendency of an object to maintain its speed, even if that speed is zero. The inertia of an object is affected by its mass. *(see also mass)*

Maglev trains are trains that use magnetic force to levitate or float above their tracks.

Magnetism is a natural force found in some metals, such as iron. *(see also magnets)*

Magnets are metals that attract other metals; usually those that contain iron. *(see also magnetism)*

Mass is the amount of substance an object has for its size. Mass causes an object to resist acceleration. *(see also inertia)*

Speed is how fast an object moves.

Streamlined means having a smooth, sleek shape that cuts easily through air, reducing air resistance. *(see also air resistance and friction)*

Tracks are the (usually) metal rails that the wheels of roller coasters roll along.

Velocity is the measurement of the combined speed and direction of an object.